Copyright © 2011 BlackButterfly Publications
All rights reserved.

ISBN-10: 0615489974
ISBN-13: 978-0615489971

Dedication

This book is dedicated to anyone who feels they have suffered in any way and has had to endure that pain whether out loud or in silence.

May you find comfort and laughter in these words knowing that you are not alone. We all have to endure moments of great sadness; unfortunately, some a little more than others.

I wish for you the courage and motivation to persevere.

Contents

Acknowledgements	i
The Glass	1
911	2
Death Becomes Her	3
To The Man Who Once Deceived Me	4
My Eyes Are Gonna Fall Outta My Head	5
Swollen Glands	6
Trapped In My Box	7
Beautiful Brown Black Woman	8
My Almond Eyes	9
Fat Girls Cry	10
Goodbye to the Butterfly	11
Bleeping	15
Scruffy McDuck	16
Stillness	17
Pity the Fool	18
The Loneliest Road in the World	19
Patience	21
Bullies	22
You and Me	23
The Only Way Up Is Down	25

Acknowledgements

I am grateful for the experiences that have inspired me to use my voice.

Thank you to anyone who supports me doing so.

The Glass

Today I've hit the glass ceiling of my potential
It is an unfortunate thing to feel at the age of 25
Somehow I peaked somewhere in childhood
Somehow my own success eluded my eyes

What a shame to tap out so young in age
No one seems to believe my defeat
They think I'm just lost or hiding myself
But honestly, this *is* my deep

How weird to feel like you're on your death bed
With nothing left to achieve
How absurd to have no more ideas or inspiration
Just waiting for your decree

If there is somehow a purpose for me
That I have yet to discover
May God grant me the will to live
So from this agony I may recover

911

Emergency Dispatcher...
Help! I'm alone
They're trying to get me
Please send someone right away
Ok, ma'am calm down
Who's trying to get you?
Tell me, what are their names?

I can't, I can't say it
There's just too many
It hurts, send help quick
This pain is unbearable
The anxiety is exhausting
And my frustration is making me sick

Ok, ma'am I want to help
But you must be honest
Tell me what you need
I need a friend
Someone to talk to
My emotions are killing me

Death Becomes Her

The one who chooses to love a boy

So naïve and irresponsible with her heart as he treats her like a toy

Death will become her

How she will love with all her heart and give up everything loving shamelessly in the dark

Silly, silly girl you say who's lost her innocence

Can't erase those scares and heal her wounds after all the men who have been

Incredibly kindhearted and unique though he sees no preciousness

Just one of many that he's meant to bang regardless of her heaven sent

Death will become her, this fragile girl so meek

So thirsty for love, so hungry for touch to trust a monster with her key

Death will become her who never learned to love herself

Who sought fulfillment in a man, clasping tighter when he hurt hoping to relieve oneself

Death becomes her to the one who didn't know herself

Too excited to care, too anxious to try who never stopped to learn her wealth

To The Man Who Once Deceived Me

To the man who once deceived me
I do not wish you harm
I'm happy for your success
 though I was once seduced by your charm

To the man who once deceived me
I smile when I see you well
I'm happy to see your dreams come true though I never fared so well

To the man who once deceived me
I do believe in karma
I hope you've learned your lesson and we heal from all the drama

To the man who once deceived me
I release you from my past
I relinquish you from my painful truth though my peace did not come as fast

To the man who once deceived me
Your behavior is forgiven
Without your apology, without your courage, and without your acknowledgment

To the man who once deceived me
I free you from my disturbance
I took the higher road and will rebuild my faith despite the company of your burdens

THE AGONY OF MY DEFEAT

My Eyes Are Gonna Fall Outta My Head

My Eyes Are Gonna Fall Outta My Head
from all the ugly they've seen witnessing so much hate
and people's spirits so mean

My Eyes Are Gonna Fall Outta My Head
because I've struggled so much been through too much heartache
and could no longer cover it up

My Eyes Are Gonna Fall Right Outta My Head
rollin' onto the floor
trying to get away from me 'cause they can't take no more

My Eyes Are Gonna Fall Outta My Head
because they've cried too many tears,
endured too many pains, and suffered injustice all these years

My Eyes Are Gonna Fall Outta My Head
cause they can't stand to cry
they've sat through prayer and fought through life yet somehow continued to die

My Eyes Are Gonna Fall Outta My Soul
revealing all my secrets left untold
God please put my eyes back in my head
and help me to see Your vision before I end up dead

Swollen Glands

Ooo child, the stress in my life
No one would believe if they knew how hard I've cried
Cried from broken hearts, cried from broken dreams but I suppose it's all the same

They say how can a pretty girl like you be so sad in life
You'd think you'd have it easy being so cute and too nice
Sorry to burst your bubble people but life hasn't been so grand
No one can escape the wrath of grief of being hurt by man

Everyone loses faith at times
Everyone stoops too low
Everybody can suffer in silence
Some just choose to gloat

Ooo child, the pains in my neck, my swollen breasts and eyes
Too much stress and not enough joy
Life has really taken me for a ride

Trapped In My Box

Trapped inside my narrow box yearning to be free
Looks okay from the outside like I'm no one in need

Scared to death of present stays, broken from my past
Hopeless about what the future holds 'cause my dreams never come to pass

Clasping, clamoring behind claustrophobic walls
Draining out my energy trying to keep them from their fall

Oh ye faithful Spirit that keeps me still alive
Fighting for my day of redemption when not an ounce of evidence lies

Trapped inside this wretched box that feels more safe, you see
Safer than the cold, harsh world
Better paralyzed than free

Beautiful Brown Black Woman

I am a beautiful brown black woman.

That is who I be.

Short, curly hair with no extensions or weaves,

A multi-tanned body with a billion acnes and scars,

A distorted vision of self with no clue of who we are,

An intelligent, inquiring mind that reflects upon the soul,

An insecure and empty heart full of un-reached goals,

A blind critical eye looks back to stare at me,

Looking for my weakness and all my disparities,

A fragile and dying soul grasping for its last breath of air,

Lingering thoughts wishing for someone who cares,

A passionate, precious soul beautifully misunderstood,

A desperate, ambitious mind trying to decipher all that it could.

A beautiful brown black woman struggling to find her place.

Define the puzzle of who she is in her imprisoned mind's state.

My Almond Eyes

To most, they are a thing of beauty with fascinating curves like angel eyes.

To others, they say they are small and squinted like Asian eyes as they ask am I Japanese.

But does anyone see deep enough, deep behind my almond brown eyes.

Can they see the well of pain inside and the stories they cannot hide?

Has anyone seen what I've seen? What my beautiful eyes mask.

Does anyone know what they know about my troubled, darkened past?

No.

They see such beautiful brown eyes.

The kind that light up when faced to the sky.

Changing colors and often bold with many stories left untold.

How they perceive my Asian eyes to even confuse my race?

They glow for show as people stare past my saddened face.

But those dear almond eyes of mine, a treasured beauty piece.

Seen all the ugly, suffered all the tears, the victims of all my grief.

K. HERU

Fat Girls Cry

Tough I am with my composed face

You can't see my pain

Stare at me if you want, I don't care

I don't feel no shame

Jiggle wiggle, yep my thighs are like thunder near the beach

Criticize my flab if you dare but your body isn't so sleek

Haters, haters on the wall

Can you talk a little louder; God didn't hear your call

Judge me, slay me with your words

Despite your lack of consciousness I'm a human and it hurts

And yet I'm strong, stronger than you

Dealt with things you could never ensue

But you don't know my story, haven't walked in my shoes

How sad is your compel to make me feel blue

Goodbye to the Butterfly

Goodbye to the Butterfly

The butterfly that never flew

Goodbye to the Butterfly

Who never knew what she should do

Goodbye to the Butterfly

Who never spread her wings

Goodbye to the Butterfly

Who never lived her dreams

Goodbye to the Butterfly

Who never found true love

Goodbye to the Butterfly

Who won't see the heavens above

Goodbye to the Butterfly

Who never found inner peace

Goodbye to the Butterfly

Who was never able to release

Goodbye to the Butterfly

Who has grown too tired and weary

Goodbye to the Butterfly

Whose eyes remain teary

K. HERU

Goodbye to the Butterfly

Who never found happiness

Say goodbye to the Butterfly

Who was finally consumed by all her stress

Goodbye to the Butterfly

Who never lived but tried

And died in the very instance that she took flight

Goodbye to the Butterfly

Who never knew her purpose or place

Who never found a friend to count on

Who never knew the joy of living

And was never able to escape

Goodbye to the Butterfly

Who never met her own needs

Goodbye to the Butterfly

Who was always found too weak

Goodbye to the Butterfly

Who never made a sound

Goodbye to the Butterfly

Whose rightful path was never found

Goodbye to the Butterfly

Who lived inside her mind

Who talked to herself and used her imagination to try to pass the time

THE AGONY OF MY DEFEAT

Goodbye to the Butterfly

Who no one would ever believe

No one cared of her struggles or gave merit to her grief

Goodbye to the Butterfly

Who was everybody's fool

Abused because unselfish and taken because it's cool

Goodbye to the Butterfly

Who could never speak,

Would never be heard or respected,

Just a lonely, lifeless, geek

Goodbye to the Butterfly

Whom no one could love

Or would ever want to

Who would cry ever night, toss and turn

From the demons that haunt through and through

Say goodbye to the Butterfly

That you never gave a chance,

That you took for granted,

Didn't appreciate, complained and talked about,

And made unruly demands

Goodbye Butterfly

I hope you find your way

To a place more beautiful from whence you just came

I hope you find a place where you can just **be,**

And finally schedule the time with God to help you find your peace

Bleeping

Hey, I've discovered my new word

Some say it's the shortest prayer

I'd have to agree that I feel a release as I blurt it with no care

Ooo shame, shame on you

You unholy freak

No I didn't mean it that way, don't pass judgment on my peace

All I'm saying is it's a nice word

To vent in times of frustration

Others may prefer to use it only in terms of consummation

Either way, it works for me

It's my new word to choose

I'll say it proudly and frequently as it needs to be used

Mercy, mercy on my soul

Forgive my crass and crude

I know it's not that lady-like but I need to do what I need to do

K. HERU

Scruffy McDuck

Scruffy McDuck

Frog-legged gorilla

I know you're not approaching me

This dirty dish rag

Scar-faced grizzly bear

Trying to act so suave and sheik

You ain't foolin' nobody

With that crust in your eyes

And that grime in your front teeth

You old dust bucket

Way out of your league

Criticizing me like I'm weak

You've got your nerve

Forcing yourself on me

And when I decline you get so rude

You've lost your sense of direction

You are out of line

Let me point you back to the zoo

Stillness

Lord, keep me still in this moment

Keep me steady in my faith

My inner thoughts are talking to me

Causing my heart to race

Lord, keep me still in this moment

Free from past's pain and future's doubts

Keep my mind from wondering

My fears speak so damn loud

Deep breath I am breathing in

Take me to that peaceful place

Silence all my insecurities

Let relaxation unhinge my face

Lord, keep me still as You talk to me

Anchoring Your words head to feet

Providing the understanding and clarity

That I so desperately need

Pity the Fool

I pity that poor young girl who sits so sad and lonely

Then brightens up her spirit the moment a man makes her feel un-homely

Only to capture what he wants

Only to possess her goods

Then dump her off the cliff of love yelling SHE misunderstood

Sad, sad day for hearts bleeding around the world

Broken dreams and promises unfulfilled for this young girl

Maybe she'll recover one day

Perhaps she won't become mean

I worry and pray for her withered soul so that she may be redeemed

THE AGONY OF MY DEFEAT

The Loneliest Road in the World

It is the road less travelled for a reason

You won't understand that until you're there

You start to question your intentions

Learning the depths of how life's unfair

It's a road made for the strong

But it will not discourage the weak

You can choose to walk it if you dare

But understand you'll be slow to peak

Victories don't come fast here

Gratification is always minimal

You'll watch others around you progress

As your thoughts begin to turn cynical

You'll try to hold tightly to your faith

Because a prayer is what you'll need

To walk this desert plank

Leaving behind vengefulness and greed

At some point you'll have to wonder

Where on earth did all the people go?

Because nobody will choose that journey with you

Because it's not a part of their growth

A depressingly lifeless road to travel

Narrowing at every bend

Where the heck does this thing turn?

I mean, seriously, is there no end?

You might see a mirage and believe it's others like you

And true, they may be good

But they'll whisk away at the hint of hardship

Leaving tears dropping down to your foot

It's a lonely road I tell you

Built for kindhearted humanitarians

Who believe in other people sometimes more than themselves

And would die seeking betterment

Patience

God please give me

Do you not know my struggles?

Have you not heard my cries?

Am I invisible to Your needs?

Patience

Oh my Lord

If you only knew my story

If you knew my journey

And could take mercy on what I've endured

Patience

I have waited

I have sat on bended knee

Cried and prayed and cried and prayed

And yet there are no seeds

Patience

Is a virtue they say

Not one many can claim

But I have waited too long to settle

God you need to get to it 'cause you are late

Bullies

Insecure little bastards

But don't you call them on it though

They'll deny it to the death turn around and judge you

Make you question what you know

Unhappy, miserable creatures

Preying on the "weak"

So bored with their own life, disappointed with their own path

It's their duty to cause you grief

Don't you point your finger at them

Don't you shine your light

They don't like their own reflection

So they try to destroy you from the inside

Try not to get discouraged

Try not to be afraid

Take a deep breath and the high road

Knowing that you come from a Higher place

You and Me

You and me

Forever to be

In each other's hearts throughout eternity

On my mind

Within my soul

I promise to love you as we grow

For the air I breathe and each day that I wake

I thank the Lord above for the blessings He creates

From the day I met you

To the beauty within your eyes

To the heaven that you bring me each day you're by my side

From the treasure of your embrace and the essence of your smile

You have brightened my life within this short while

Please take my hand as we pray for peace, for love, and honor of each other's needs.

I share with you my heart.

I give to you my soul.

I protect you with my spirit and my angels tenfold.

You are my precious, my incandescent light.

It is only for you that I will shine this bright

You and me

Now as I speak,

In each other's lives waiting for our destiny

Try as we might

Step out on faith

Taking a chance in fear of mistakes

As we question our fate, and grow in our love,

We put our trust in the Lord above.

May He guide us with peace and shower us with grace

May we learn from our experiences and find forgiveness in place.

Lord give us the strength and the courage each day.

May we learn to appreciate each blessing you gave.

I thank you for his spirit.

I am grateful for his heart.

May we let nothing and no one tear us apart.

THE AGONY OF MY DEFEAT

The Only Way Up Is Down

Sometimes in life we find that the only way to get up is to be knocked down

The only way to smile is through frowns

The only way we can continue to live is to lounge

Sometimes in life the only way to get in is to get out

The only way to be heard is to shout

And the only way we learn to believe is to doubt

Sometimes in life we find that the only way to feel is to hurt

The only way to want is to yearn

And the only way to cry is to burn

Sometimes in life we have to fall

It's the only way we learn our resolve

It's how we find out who we can really call

Sometimes in life the only way we win is to suffer defeat

And the time we find our love, we cheat

And the moment we've given up, we are released

Sometimes in life our perfection is imperfect

We find our troubles are just not worth it

And giving in is where the hurt is

Sometimes in life the ups must come down

To learn to swim, we have to drown

And to create our voices from once no sound

"The BlackButterfly is the most beautiful and resilient creature, full of an undying faith in what is good and flying with a persistence of hope."

~ K. Heru